THE
PAPA SUTRA[1]

by

Rev. Dr. Richard E. Kuykendall
Photography by Andrew Kuykendall

Order this book online at www.trafford.com
or email orders@trafford.com

Most Trafford titles are also available at major online book retailers.

 www.trafford.com

North America & international
toll-free: 844 688 6899 (USA & Canada)
fax: 812 355 4082

Our mission is to efficiently provide the world's finest, most comprehensive book publishing service, enabling every author to experience success. To find out how to publish your book, your way, and have it available worldwide, visit us online at www.trafford.com

ISBN: 978-1-6987-1896-5 (sc)
ISBN: 978-1-6987-1897-2 (e)

Library of Congress Control Number: 2025903089

Print information available on the last page.

Trafford rev. 02/19/2025

Dedicated to
Bowen Lee Kendrick
the second Baby Buddha,
and my daughter
Leah Kendrick

BABBY

BUDDHA 2

In this book are some of the things your Papa has learned over the years. I hope these things will make your life easier and that they will help you be more happy and at peace.

First, be thankful for your mother and your father and other family members. And also be thankful for the earth with its rocks and mountains, and rivers, lakes, and the sea. Be thankful for the fish and the birds, the lizards and frogs and all the animals—and even the insects. And if you feel you are too small to do anything, just think of what even a mosquito can do—make a grown up scratch!

Long, long, ago, in a land far away, a son was born to a king and queen. As the boy grew, he had everything and anything he wanted. But having everything didn't really give him peace. And so one day, after he had grown up, he left his father and mother's palace, and went into the forest to seek the truth of why life is the way it is, and how to live one's life.

And do you know what? After seven years, the boy--who was now a man, quit searching and just sat down under a tree and said, "I will not get up from this spot until I know the truth of why life is the way it is, and how I should live my life."

The man sat under the tree without eating anything for many days, and during that time there were times when he was hungry, and times he was scared, and times he was angry, and times he was sad, BUT he never let those feelings keep him from only wanting the answer to his questions, "Why is life the way it is, and how should I live my life?"

And after over a month of sitting there under the tree he got his answer. And this is what he learned, as to, "Why life is the way that it is, and how should one live their life?"

The first thing he learned was: even though we live in a beautiful world full of beautiful things--just think of all the beautiful things you can see, hear, smell, taste, and feel... and yet there is also pain and sorrow.

And strange as it may seem, our desire to have no pain is what gives us even more pain. So the question is: "How can we stop the pain and sorrow?" And even the answer to this came to the man under the tree:

And the answer that came to him was that though there is no way to remove all pain and sorrow from our lives, this is the way you can avoid a great deal of it, and it is therefore how we should live our lives:

1. Don't hurt people.

2.	Always be kind.

3. Don't take things that don't belong to you.

4. Always tell the truth.[2]

5. Always do the best that you can.

If you do these five things you will live a happier and more loving life for yourself and those around you. And if everyone would do these things the world would be at peace once and for all.

If at this point you feel that I have not answered all of your questions, consider this:

Once a student of the Buddha asked him the following questions:

1. "Is their a God?
2. "What was before the universe began?"
3. "Is the universe infinite in both space and time?"
4. "Do humans have *souls* which survive death of the body?"
5. If humans survive death, in what form would they be in and where would they be?"

These are what the Buddha called the, "Unknowables"--questions that the Buddha believed were unknowable, and he taught this parable to make his point:

"If a man is wounded by an arrow with the point covered with poison, he doesn't ask questions like what kind of wood is the arrow made of, and what is the substance of the arrowhead, nor what kind of poison is on the point of the arrow. These questions are meaningless. Instead, he simply needs to have the arrow taken out."

This being said, just for you I will share my answers to these "Unknowables." And though I cannot prove them, I think I can give good reasons for my beliefs. So here we go...

"Is their a God?"

The first of these questions had to do with God. First you need to know that people from all over the world, and in all times have believed in various gods and goddesses. For instance, there were the Greek gods and goddesses of Mount Olympus—with Zeus as the head of all of the gods and goddesses and Hera his goddess wife. To the south of the Greeks were the Egyptians with their Isis and Osiris, and many other gods and goddesses, and to the north there were the Nordic gods and goddesses with Odin as the head.

ZEUS

OSIRIS

ODIN

FRIGG

HERA

ISIS

21

These people all believed that there were many gods and goddesses, but then came those who believed in only One god. These are found among the Jews, the Christians, and the Muslims.

Then there are those who believe that God is everything.

But if you were to ask me what I believe about God, this is what I would say...

"Everything came from
God, and is in God,
and
God is in all things."[3]

Another question about God is, how can we know God, or where do we find evidence of God?

My answer is, one way is "an inner knowing" which is something one experiences. Many have offered the evidence of design in the universe, and nature on the earth, with its many life forms. To me, despite what those who don't believe say, I don't believe that its all just an accident!

Finally, there is the evidence of nature itself...creation to me needs a Creator—it just didn't come together randomly and accidentally by itself —and yet the problem of why there is so much suffering, if the "Creator" was benevolent still hangs over us like a dark cloud.

Then there is the question about the *gender* of god.

Though in the past there were many gods and goddesses; in the religions where people believed in only one god, they believed god was male—a Father God—with no female god or goddesses. And so many people pray to God the Father. In the 1980s however, there was a revival of the Goddess in the Goddess Movement, and even in some Christian churches they began to pray saying, "Dear Mother/Father God..."

Now the bottom line is that God is not a male or a female (that would imply male and female body parts which is just silly to think); as Jesus said, "God is Spirit"--and in fact, I believe that God is everywhere present. In other words, there is no place where God is not there.

"What was before the universe began?"

As for the question of "What was before the universe began?" To this you could add, "What was before God?" My answer therefore to both is that both God and the universe have always been, and they not only have no beginning, they also have no end.

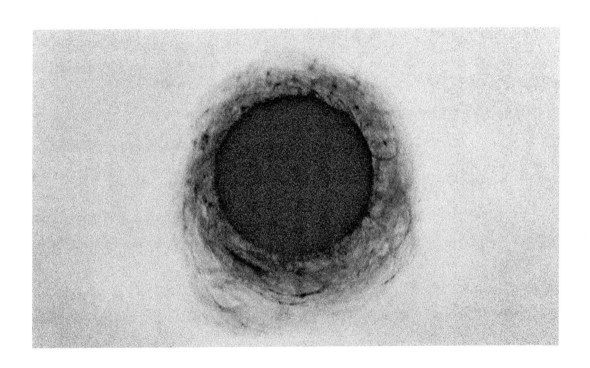

"Is the universe infinite in both space and time?"

It follows from the answer to our earlier question, "Yes, both God and the universe are infinite, or eternal.

"Do humans have *souls* which survive death of the body?"

Though I admit there is no solid proof that the soul survives the death of the body. And yet every culture from all times in history believed or believes in this—from ancient humans who buried their dead in the earth in fetal positions, and covered them with red ocher, as if preparing them for rebirth, to Egyptians with their mummies, to modern stories of near-death experiences. I know that skeptics say that the fact that the vast majority of the world, from all times, have believed in life after death, does NOT constitute as proof. Well, skeptics cannot prove that we do not survive death.

"If humans survive death, in what form would they be in and where would they be?"

There are a number of ways that various religions have understood how humans survive death. Here are just a few: Reincarnation, where the soul is reborn in another body to finish their work. Immortality of the soul where one dies and their souls go to "Heaven" or "Hell." Soul sleep (R. I. P.) until the resurrection day, when the souls are reunited with their bodies and go to Heaven or Hell. Or another view is that when we die our souls are united with God.

And so, I'm sure you will have even more questions than these. But I have written many books in which you will find even more answers. So goodbye for now and know that your Papa loves you and wants to pass on to you what I have learned. May God bless you and your family as they do their best to raise you.

(Endnotes)

1 A Sutra is a Buddhist scripture. The word Sutra in Sanskrit literally means, "Thread"-- some think this referred to the thread that that was used to hold "books" together, or the tread that holds the religious teachings together.

2 By truth I do not mean to say that if someone asks you how they look, and you think they look horrible—its better to says something like, "You look just fine," or "Its you!" and let it go at that. No one's life depends on hurting someone's feelings.. My example for this always is: "If you were a German in Nazi Germany, and were hiding your best friends because they were Jewish, if the Gestapos knocked on your door demanding the surrender of any Jews—would you say, "Yes, they are hiding up in the attic.." Or would you say, "I'm sorry but there are none h ere." But this kind of discussion is for older children, probably in most cases at least in middle school.

3 How I like to say this is as follows: "God is the name I give to the source and essence of all that is."

Printed in the United States
by Baker & Taylor Publisher Services